Dedicated to:

- All who wish to "Up Their Game" with healthy, daily self-care routines.

- Anyone seeking to better themselves and rise into their greatest potential.

- All who desire to create a healthier self in order to serve humanity with that healthier self.

Other Publications by this Author:

The Voyage: Finding the Beautiful Gems of My Being

The Voyage: All Age Coloring Book

Volume 1- Positive Quotes with Author Holly

30 day Gratitude/JOY Pocket Journal

Volume 2- Positive Quotes with Author Holly

90 day Gratitude/JOY Pocket Journal

90 day Daily Self-Care Accountability Logbook

90 day Daily Self-Care Accountability Log/Reflect Journal

30 day Daily Self-Care Accountability Logbook

Volume 3- Positive Quotes with Author Holly

Joyful Navigations

30 day
Daily Self-Care

Accountability Logbook

and

Reflection Journal

Holly Ruttenbur Dickinson
Foreword by
Robert L. Bray, PhD, LCSW, TFT-VT

30 day, Daily Self-Care Accountability Logbook and Reflection Journal by Holly Ruttenbur Dickinson.

A self-care logbook and reflection journal.

Copyright ©2020 Holly Ruttenbur Dickinson
Joyful Navigations/Trade Name
Joyful Navigations™
Published by Shifting Open LLC.

Self-Help, Personal Growth, Happiness, Best Self, Well-being, Joy, Joyful, Accountability, Self-Management, Health, Soul

Book Design, Graphics, Logbook Design by Holly Dickinson. Foreword by Robert L. Bray PhD, LCSW, TFT-VT.

Printed in the United States of America

Visit me on the Facebook Page: *Positive Quotes with Author Holly* and *Choose Joyful with Joyful Navigations*™
Website: https://joyfulnavigations.com

ISBN: 978-1-7355347-9-4

Table of Contents

I acknowledge that as I take better care of me, I am happier and more filled with JOY and peace.

For a better world... It starts with how we treat ourselves.

Affirmation:
Self-care is VITAL, in order for ME to RISE into my GREATEST potential.

Work on yourself, to become your BEST self. And... be KIND and LOVING to yourself.

You may not like my process, my way, but it works for me. I've learned, at great cost, that I have to put me first, then I can serve others.

I always served humanity first and put me last. That's what society taught me. It caused body sickness. I've had to learn a different way that isn't popular...Self-Care. I'm hoping to teach you to take good care of yourself FIRST, so you can better care for humanity. It needs to be taught that self-care isn't a "bad" thing, but that it's a NECESSARY daily routine for a healthy mind and healthy body. If you don't put gas in a car, at some point it will stop working. The daily routine of self-care is like putting gas into your car so it will work properly. It is CRITICAL.

Holly Ruttenbur Dickinson Self-Care Quotes

Self-Care is...

To understand that YOU are crucial to your OWN well being. This is something that is not widely taught or accepted. However, I've come to understand its great truth. It's important to realize and understand that YOU are the FIRST part of your own equation of happiness, of JOY. If you leave yourself out, you will ALWAYS be empty. Being empty is not self-care, self-love, or self-nurturing. Then, take the necessary steps to care for your health and well-being (mind, body, spirit) each day. Nurture yourself. You are your greatest care. How you speak to yourself, how you treat yourself, how you nurture yourself and build yourself up, are all a part of loving self-care. You must love YOU in order to be happy. YOU need YOU, more than you need anyone!!! (I'm not talking about God/Source/Divine/Universe. I'm speaking of humans.) You cannot be disconnected from yourself in true happiness, in true JOY!!

To change YOUR life, your habits, or your direction... It takes Awareness, then a Decision, then Action!

I'm, "in better service" for you, when I'm taking good care of me.

~Foreword~

Observing something changes it. This is true in all aspects of our existence. Reflecting on your personal daily routine of physical, mental, emotional, and spiritual actions will change you. This little logbook is a way to observe your self-care over time. Awareness is the first step in change. Seeing what you write down about what you are doing will change what you do. Ms. Holly Ruttenbur Dickinson's life has changed for the good by her paying close attention to her routines, feelings, interactions, and intentions. Her focus on the positive aspects of living and growing in joy is an inspiration to anyone committed to being one's best self in all aspects of life. Using this tool moves you towards Joy, Love, Gratitude, Peace, Compassion, Kindness, Courage and makes a better world for us all.

Robert L Bray, PhD, LCSW, TFT-VT

Notes:

_____
_____
_____
_____
_____
_____
_____
_____
_____
_____
_____
_____
_____
_____
_____
_____
_____
_____
_____
_____
_____
_____

Suggested Daily Self-Care Process

- Keep the logbook next to your bed or where you do your wake up self-care routine. Or Keep it in your day bag where it can be close to your fingertips for quick access during times of the day you know you will be able to log.

- Allow the daily practice to be a priority in order to shift to a healthier way of BEing. **This logbook is a tool to assist you in becoming accountable to yourself; for taking better care of yourself.**

- **This reflection Journal is a tool** to assist you in focusing on the lessons and the gems within everything you experience. Everything! Whether joyful of painful, the lessons and the gems are there. Through daily reflection journaling, you'll be able to discover them and use them, to level up to more of your potential. This process can assist in looking for the positive in each of life's challenges.

- If you miss a day, just resume on the next day. **Avoid being critical of yourself** if you miss a day here and there. In fact, show yourself more tenderness and love and loving self-talk when you fall short of your own expectations. It takes time and consistent effort to create a new habit/routine.

- The date is left blank for you to fill in on your schedule. The more often you do this as a daily routine, the faster it will become a healthy self-care habit.

- Just by purchasing this logbook and journal, it shows that you are willing to take steps to help yourself become a better you, a healthier you, and transform your life. I'm excited for YOU!

Notes:

_____

_____

_____

_____

_____

_____

_____

_____

_____

_____

_____

_____

_____

_____

Date _____   _____

Supplements/Vitamins/Medications:

_____

Fitness/Cardio: (30 min suggested)

_____

Deep Breathing/Body Stretching/Laughing:

_____

Spirituality: (Meditation/Prayer etc)

_____

Mind/Brain: (Reading/Writing/Journaling etc)

_____

Nature or Green Space:

_____

Hydration: (how much?)

_____

Sleep: (6-8 hours suggested)(How long?)

_____

Self-Tenderness/Self-Nurturing: (Self-hug and say I love you, to you!, Say kind things to self)

_____

Positive Mindset/Manifesting Practices: (Gratitude Journaling/Affirmations/Vision Board etc)

_____

Other Self-Care: (Example: doctor visit, pedicure, relaxed, baseball game, time with friends, time with pet)

_____

_____

Today's Reflection: (Focus on lessons & gems)

_____

_____

_____

_____

_____

_____

_____

_____

_____

_____

_____

_____

_____

_____

_____

_____

_____

_____

_____

_____

_____

_____

_____

Date _____   _____

Supplements/Vitamins/Medications:

_____

_____
Fitness/Cardio: (30 min suggested)

_____
Deep Breathing/Body Stretching/Laughing:

_____
Spirituality: (Meditation/Prayer etc)

_____
Mind/Brain: (Reading/Writing/Journaling etc)

_____
Nature or Green Space:

_____
Hydration: (how much?)

_____
Sleep: (6-8 hours suggested)(How long?)

_____
Self-Tenderness/Self-Nurturing: (Self-hug and say I love you, to you!, Say kind things to self)

_____
Positive Mindset/Manifesting Practices: (Gratitude Journaling/Affirmations/Vision Board etc)

_____
Other Self-Care: (Example: doctor visit, pedicure, relaxed, baseball game, time with friends, time with pet)

_____

_____

Today's Reflection: (Focus on lessons & gems)

_____

_____

_____

_____

_____

_____

_____

_____

_____

_____

_____

_____

_____

_____

_____

_____

_____

_____

_____

_____

Date _____   _____

Supplements/Vitamins/Medications:
_____
_____
Fitness/Cardio: (30 min suggested)
_____
Deep Breathing/Body Stretching/Laughing:
_____
Spirituality: (Meditation/Prayer etc)
_____
Mind/Brain: (Reading/Writing/Journaling etc)
_____
Nature or Green Space:
_____
Hydration: (how much?)
_____
Sleep: (6-8 hours suggested)(How long?)
_____
Self-Tenderness/Self-Nurturing: (Self-hug and
say I love you, to you!, Say kind things to self)
_____
Positive Mindset/Manifesting Practices:
(Gratitude Journaling/Affirmations/Vision
Board etc)
_____
Other Self-Care: (Example: doctor visit,
pedicure, relaxed, baseball game, time with
friends, time with pet)
_____
_____

Today's Reflection: (Focus on lessons & gems)

_____

_____

_____

_____

_____

_____

_____

_____

_____

_____

_____

_____

_____

_____

_____

_____

_____

_____

_____

_____

_____

_____

_____

Date _____   _____

Supplements/Vitamins/Medications:
_____
_____

Fitness/Cardio: (30 min suggested)
_____

Deep Breathing/Body Stretching/Laughing:
_____

Spirituality: (Meditation/Prayer etc)
_____

Mind/Brain: (Reading/Writing/Journaling etc)
_____

Nature or Green Space:
_____

Hydration: (how much?)
_____

Sleep: (6-8 hours suggested)(How long?)
_____

Self-Tenderness/Self-Nurturing: (Self-hug and say I love you, to you!, Say kind things to self)
_____

Positive Mindset/Manifesting Practices: (Gratitude Journaling/Affirmations/Vision Board etc)
_____

Other Self-Care: (Example: doctor visit, pedicure, relaxed, baseball game, time with friends, time with pet)

_____
_____

Today's Reflection: (Focus on lessons & gems)

_____

_____

_____

_____

_____

_____

_____

_____

_____

_____

_____

_____

_____

_____

_____

_____

_____

_____

_____

_____

_____

Date _____   _____

Supplements/Vitamins/Medications:

_____

Fitness/Cardio: (30 min suggested)

_____

Deep Breathing/Body Stretching/Laughing:

_____

Spirituality: (Meditation/Prayer etc)

_____

Mind/Brain: (Reading/Writing/Journaling etc)

_____

Nature or Green Space:

_____

Hydration: (how much?)

_____

Sleep: (6-8 hours suggested)(How long?)

_____

Self-Tenderness/Self-Nurturing: (Self-hug and
say I love you, to you!, Say kind things to self)

_____

Positive Mindset/Manifesting Practices:
(Gratitude Journaling/Affirmations/Vision
Board etc)

_____

Other Self-Care: (Example: doctor visit,
pedicure, relaxed, baseball game, time with
friends, time with pet)

_____

_____

Today's Reflection: (Focus on lessons & gems)

_____

_____

_____

_____

_____

_____

_____

_____

_____

_____

_____

_____

_____

_____

_____

_____

_____

_____

_____

_____

_____

_____

_____

Date _____ _____

Supplements/Vitamins/Medications:

_____

_____
Fitness/Cardio: (30 min suggested)

_____
Deep Breathing/Body Stretching/Laughing:

_____
Spirituality: (Meditation/Prayer etc)

_____
Mind/Brain: (Reading/Writing/Journaling etc)

_____
Nature or Green Space:

_____
Hydration: (how much?)

_____
Sleep: (6-8 hours suggested)(How long?)

_____
Self-Tenderness/Self-Nurturing: (Self-hug and
say I love you, to you!, Say kind things to self)

_____
Positive Mindset/Manifesting Practices:
(Gratitude Journaling/Affirmations/Vision
Board etc)

_____
Other Self-Care: (Example: doctor visit,
pedicure, relaxed, baseball game, time with
friends, time with pet)

_____

_____

Today's Reflection: (Focus on lessons & gems)

_____
_____
_____
_____
_____
_____
_____
_____
_____
_____
_____
_____
_____
_____
_____
_____
_____
_____
_____
_____
_____
_____
_____

Date _____   _____

Supplements/Vitamins/Medications:

_____
_____

Fitness/Cardio: (30 min suggested)

_____

Deep Breathing/Body Stretching/Laughing:

_____

Spirituality: (Meditation/Prayer etc)

_____

Mind/Brain: (Reading/Writing/Journaling etc)

_____

Nature or Green Space:

_____

Hydration: (how much?)

_____

Sleep: (6-8 hours suggested)(How long?)

_____

Self-Tenderness/Self-Nurturing: (Self-hug and say I love you, to you!, Say kind things to self)

_____

Positive Mindset/Manifesting Practices: (Gratitude Journaling/Affirmations/Vision Board etc)

_____

Other Self-Care: (Example: doctor visit, pedicure, relaxed, baseball game, time with friends, time with pet)

_____
_____

Today's Reflection: (Focus on lessons & gems)

_____

_____

_____

_____

_____

_____

_____

_____

_____

_____

_____

_____

_____

_____

_____

_____

_____

_____

_____

_____

_____

Date _____   _____

Supplements/Vitamins/Medications:
_____
_____

Fitness/Cardio: (30 min suggested)
_____

Deep Breathing/Body Stretching/Laughing:
_____

Spirituality: (Meditation/Prayer etc)
_____

Mind/Brain: (Reading/Writing/Journaling etc)
_____

Nature or Green Space:
_____

Hydration: (how much?)
_____

Sleep: (6-8 hours suggested)(How long?)
_____

Self-Tenderness/Self-Nurturing: (Self-hug and say I love you, to you!, Say kind things to self)
_____

Positive Mindset/Manifesting Practices: (Gratitude Journaling/Affirmations/Vision Board etc)
_____

Other Self-Care: (Example: doctor visit, pedicure, relaxed, baseball game, time with friends, time with pet)
_____
_____

Today's Reflection: (Focus on lessons & gems)

_____

_____

_____

_____

_____

_____

_____

_____

_____

_____

_____

_____

_____

_____

_____

_____

_____

_____

_____

_____

_____

Date _____   _____

Supplements/Vitamins/Medications:
_____
_____

Fitness/Cardio: (30 min suggested)
_____

Deep Breathing/Body Stretching/Laughing:
_____

Spirituality: (Meditation/Prayer etc)
_____

Mind/Brain: (Reading/Writing/Journaling etc)
_____

Nature or Green Space:
_____

Hydration: (how much?)
_____

Sleep: (6-8 hours suggested)(How long?)
_____

Self-Tenderness/Self-Nurturing: (Self-hug and say I love you, to you!, Say kind things to self)
_____

Positive Mindset/Manifesting Practices: (Gratitude Journaling/Affirmations/Vision Board etc)
_____

Other Self-Care: (Example: doctor visit, pedicure, relaxed, baseball game, time with friends, time with pet)

_____
_____

Today's Reflection: (Focus on lessons & gems)

_____

_____

_____

_____

_____

_____

_____

_____

_____

_____

_____

_____

_____

_____

_____

_____

_____

_____

_____

_____

_____

_____

_____

Date _____   _____

Supplements/Vitamins/Medications:
_____
_____

Fitness/Cardio: (30 min suggested)
_____

Deep Breathing/Body Stretching/Laughing:
_____

Spirituality: (Meditation/Prayer etc)
_____

Mind/Brain: (Reading/Writing/Journaling etc)
_____

Nature or Green Space:
_____

Hydration: (how much?)
_____

Sleep: (6-8 hours suggested)(How long?)
_____

Self-Tenderness/Self-Nurturing: (Self-hug and
say I love you, to you!, Say kind things to self)
_____

Positive Mindset/Manifesting Practices:
(Gratitude Journaling/Affirmations/Vision
Board etc)
_____

Other Self-Care: (Example: doctor visit,
pedicure, relaxed, baseball game, time with
friends, time with pet)

_____
_____

Today's Reflection: (Focus on lessons & gems)

_____

_____

_____

_____

_____

_____

_____

_____

_____

_____

_____

_____

_____

_____

_____

_____

_____

_____

_____

_____

_____

_____

_____

Date _____   _____

Supplements/Vitamins/Medications:

_____

_____

Fitness/Cardio: (30 min suggested)

_____

Deep Breathing/Body Stretching/Laughing:

_____

Spirituality: (Meditation/Prayer etc)

_____

Mind/Brain: (Reading/Writing/Journaling etc)

_____

Nature or Green Space:

_____

Hydration: (how much?)

_____

Sleep: (6-8 hours suggested)(How long?)

_____

Self-Tenderness/Self-Nurturing: (Self-hug and
say I love you, to you!, Say kind things to self)

_____

Positive Mindset/Manifesting Practices:
(Gratitude Journaling/Affirmations/Vision
Board etc)

_____

Other Self-Care: (Example: doctor visit,
pedicure, relaxed, baseball game, time with
friends, time with pet)

_____

_____

Today's Reflection: (Focus on lessons & gems)

_____

_____

_____

_____

_____

_____

_____

_____

_____

_____

_____

_____

_____

_____

_____

_____

_____

_____

_____

_____

Date _____   _____

Supplements/Vitamins/Medications:

_____

_____

Fitness/Cardio: (30 min suggested)

_____

Deep Breathing/Body Stretching/Laughing:

_____

Spirituality: (Meditation/Prayer etc)

_____

Mind/Brain: (Reading/Writing/Journaling etc)

_____

Nature or Green Space:

_____

Hydration: (how much?)

_____

Sleep: (6-8 hours suggested)(How long?)

_____

Self-Tenderness/Self-Nurturing: (Self-hug and say I love you, to you!, Say kind things to self)

_____

Positive Mindset/Manifesting Practices: (Gratitude Journaling/Affirmations/Vision Board etc)

_____

Other Self-Care: (Example: doctor visit, pedicure, relaxed, baseball game, time with friends, time with pet)

_____

_____

Today's Reflection: (Focus on lessons & gems)

_____

_____

_____

_____

_____

_____

_____

_____

_____

_____

_____

_____

_____

_____

_____

_____

_____

_____

_____

_____

_____

Date _____   _____

Supplements/Vitamins/Medications:
_____
_____

Fitness/Cardio: (30 min suggested)
_____

Deep Breathing/Body Stretching/Laughing:
_____

Spirituality: (Meditation/Prayer etc)
_____

Mind/Brain: (Reading/Writing/Journaling etc)
_____

Nature or Green Space:
_____

Hydration: (how much?)
_____

Sleep: (6-8 hours suggested)(How long?)
_____

Self-Tenderness/Self-Nurturing: (Self-hug and
say I love you, to you!, Say kind things to self)
_____

Positive Mindset/Manifesting Practices:
(Gratitude Journaling/Affirmations/Vision
Board etc)
_____

Other Self-Care: (Example: doctor visit,
pedicure, relaxed, baseball game, time with
friends, time with pet)
_____
_____

Today's Reflection: (Focus on lessons & gems)

_____
_____
_____
_____
_____
_____
_____
_____
_____
_____
_____
_____
_____
_____
_____
_____
_____
_____
_____
_____
_____
_____
_____
_____

Date _____   _____

Supplements/Vitamins/Medications:

_____

_____
Fitness/Cardio: (30 min suggested)

_____
Deep Breathing/Body Stretching/Laughing:

_____
Spirituality: (Meditation/Prayer etc)

_____
Mind/Brain: (Reading/Writing/Journaling etc)

_____
Nature or Green Space:

_____
Hydration: (how much?)

_____
Sleep: (6-8 hours suggested)(How long?)

_____
Self-Tenderness/Self-Nurturing: (Self-hug and
say I love you, to you!, Say kind things to self)

_____
Positive Mindset/Manifesting Practices:
(Gratitude Journaling/Affirmations/Vision
Board etc)

_____
Other Self-Care: (Example: doctor visit,
pedicure, relaxed, baseball game, time with
friends, time with pet)

_____

_____

Today's Reflection: (Focus on lessons & gems)

_____

_____

_____

_____

_____

_____

_____

_____

_____

_____

_____

_____

_____

_____

_____

_____

_____

_____

_____

_____

_____

Date _____   _____

Supplements/Vitamins/Medications:

_____

_____
Fitness/Cardio: (30 min suggested)

_____
Deep Breathing/Body Stretching/Laughing:

_____
Spirituality: (Meditation/Prayer etc)

_____
Mind/Brain: (Reading/Writing/Journaling etc)

_____
Nature or Green Space:

_____
Hydration: (how much?)

_____
Sleep: (6-8 hours suggested)(How long?)

_____
Self-Tenderness/Self-Nurturing: (Self-hug and
say I love you, to you!, Say kind things to self)

_____
Positive Mindset/Manifesting Practices:
(Gratitude Journaling/Affirmations/Vision
Board etc)

_____
Other Self-Care: (Example: doctor visit,
pedicure, relaxed, baseball game, time with
friends, time with pet)

_____

_____

Today's Reflection: (Focus on lessons & gems)

_____

_____

_____

_____

_____

_____

_____

_____

_____

_____

_____

_____

_____

_____

_____

_____

_____

_____

_____

_____

_____

Date _____ _____

Supplements/Vitamins/Medications:
_____
_____

Fitness/Cardio: (30 min suggested)
_____

Deep Breathing/Body Stretching/Laughing:
_____

Spirituality: (Meditation/Prayer etc)
_____

Mind/Brain: (Reading/Writing/Journaling etc)
_____

Nature or Green Space:
_____

Hydration: (how much?)
_____

Sleep: (6-8 hours suggested)(How long?)
_____

Self-Tenderness/Self-Nurturing: (Self-hug and say I love you, to you!, Say kind things to self)
_____

Positive Mindset/Manifesting Practices: (Gratitude Journaling/Affirmations/Vision Board etc)
_____

Other Self-Care: (Example: doctor visit, pedicure, relaxed, baseball game, time with friends, time with pet)

_____
_____

Today's Reflection: (Focus on lessons & gems)

_____

_____

_____

_____

_____

_____

_____

_____

_____

_____

_____

_____

_____

_____

_____

_____

_____

_____

_____

_____

_____

_____

Date _____   _____

Supplements/Vitamins/Medications:

_____

_____

Fitness/Cardio: (30 min suggested)

_____

Deep Breathing/Body Stretching/Laughing:

_____

Spirituality: (Meditation/Prayer etc)

_____

Mind/Brain: (Reading/Writing/Journaling etc)

_____

Nature or Green Space:

_____

Hydration: (how much?)

_____

Sleep: (6-8 hours suggested)(How long?)

_____

Self-Tenderness/Self-Nurturing: (Self-hug and say I love you, to you!, Say kind things to self)

_____

Positive Mindset/Manifesting Practices: (Gratitude Journaling/Affirmations/Vision Board etc)

_____

Other Self-Care: (Example: doctor visit, pedicure, relaxed, baseball game, time with friends, time with pet)

_____

_____

Today's Reflection: (Focus on lessons & gems)

_____

_____

_____

_____

_____

_____

_____

_____

_____

_____

_____

_____

_____

_____

_____

_____

_____

_____

_____

_____

_____

_____

Date _____   _____

Supplements/Vitamins/Medications:
_____
_____
Fitness/Cardio: (30 min suggested)
_____
Deep Breathing/Body Stretching/Laughing:
_____
Spirituality: (Meditation/Prayer etc)
_____
Mind/Brain: (Reading/Writing/Journaling etc)
_____
Nature or Green Space:
_____
Hydration: (how much?)
_____
Sleep: (6-8 hours suggested)(How long?)
_____
Self-Tenderness/Self-Nurturing: (Self-hug and say I love you, to you!, Say kind things to self)
_____
Positive Mindset/Manifesting Practices: (Gratitude Journaling/Affirmations/Vision Board etc)
_____
Other Self-Care: (Example: doctor visit, pedicure, relaxed, baseball game, time with friends, time with pet)
_____
_____

Today's Reflection: (Focus on lessons & gems)

_____

_____

_____

_____

_____

_____

_____

_____

_____

_____

_____

_____

_____

_____

_____

_____

_____

_____

_____

_____

_____

_____

Date _____   _____

Supplements/Vitamins/Medications:
_____
_____

Fitness/Cardio: (30 min suggested)
_____

Deep Breathing/Body Stretching/Laughing:
_____

Spirituality: (Meditation/Prayer etc)
_____

Mind/Brain: (Reading/Writing/Journaling etc)
_____

Nature or Green Space:
_____

Hydration: (how much?)
_____

Sleep: (6-8 hours suggested)(How long?)
_____

Self-Tenderness/Self-Nurturing: (Self-hug and
say I love you, to you!, Say kind things to self)
_____

Positive Mindset/Manifesting Practices:
(Gratitude Journaling/Affirmations/Vision
Board etc)
_____

Other Self-Care: (Example: doctor visit,
pedicure, relaxed, baseball game, time with
friends, time with pet)

_____
_____

Today's Reflection: (Focus on lessons & gems)

_____

_____

_____

_____

_____

_____

_____

_____

_____

_____

_____

_____

_____

_____

_____

_____

_____

_____

_____

_____

_____

_____

_____

Date _____   _____

Supplements/Vitamins/Medications:

_____
_____

Fitness/Cardio: (30 min suggested)

_____

Deep Breathing/Body Stretching/Laughing:

_____

Spirituality: (Meditation/Prayer etc)

_____

Mind/Brain: (Reading/Writing/Journaling etc)

_____

Nature or Green Space:

_____

Hydration: (how much?)

_____

Sleep: (6-8 hours suggested)(How long?)

_____

Self-Tenderness/Self-Nurturing: (Self-hug and say I love you, to you!, Say kind things to self)

_____

Positive Mindset/Manifesting Practices: (Gratitude Journaling/Affirmations/Vision Board etc)

_____

Other Self-Care: (Example: doctor visit, pedicure, relaxed, baseball game, time with friends, time with pet)

_____
_____

Today's Reflection: (Focus on lessons & gems)

_____

_____

_____

_____

_____

_____

_____

_____

_____

_____

_____

_____

_____

_____

_____

_____

_____

_____

_____

_____

_____

_____

Date _____   _____

Supplements/Vitamins/Medications:
_____
_____

Fitness/Cardio: (30 min suggested)
_____

Deep Breathing/Body Stretching/Laughing:
_____

Spirituality: (Meditation/Prayer etc)
_____

Mind/Brain: (Reading/Writing/Journaling etc)
_____

Nature or Green Space:
_____

Hydration: (how much?)
_____

Sleep: (6-8 hours suggested)(How long?)
_____

Self-Tenderness/Self-Nurturing: (Self-hug and
say I love you, to you!, Say kind things to self)
_____

Positive Mindset/Manifesting Practices:
(Gratitude Journaling/Affirmations/Vision
Board etc)
_____

Other Self-Care: (Example: doctor visit,
pedicure, relaxed, baseball game, time with
friends, time with pet)

_____
_____

Today's Reflection: (Focus on lessons & gems)

_____

_____

_____

_____

_____

_____

_____

_____

_____

_____

_____

_____

_____

_____

_____

_____

_____

_____

_____

_____

_____

_____

Date _____   _____

Supplements/Vitamins/Medications:
_____
_____

Fitness/Cardio: (30 min suggested)
_____

Deep Breathing/Body Stretching/Laughing:
_____

Spirituality: (Meditation/Prayer etc)
_____

Mind/Brain: (Reading/Writing/Journaling etc)
_____

Nature or Green Space:
_____

Hydration: (how much?)
_____

Sleep: (6-8 hours suggested)(How long?)
_____

Self-Tenderness/Self-Nurturing: (Self-hug and
say I love you, to you!, Say kind things to self)
_____

Positive Mindset/Manifesting Practices:
(Gratitude Journaling/Affirmations/Vision
Board etc)
_____

Other Self-Care: (Example: doctor visit,
pedicure, relaxed, baseball game, time with
friends, time with pet)
_____
_____

Today's Reflection: (Focus on lessons & gems)

_____

_____

_____

_____

_____

_____

_____

_____

_____

_____

_____

_____

_____

_____

_____

_____

_____

_____

_____

_____

_____

Date _____   _____

Supplements/Vitamins/Medications:
_____
_____

Fitness/Cardio: (30 min suggested)
_____

Deep Breathing/Body Stretching/Laughing:
_____

Spirituality: (Meditation/Prayer etc)
_____

Mind/Brain: (Reading/Writing/Journaling etc)
_____

Nature or Green Space:
_____

Hydration: (how much?)
_____

Sleep: (6-8 hours suggested)(How long?)
_____

Self-Tenderness/Self-Nurturing: (Self-hug and
say I love you, to you!, Say kind things to self)
_____

Positive Mindset/Manifesting Practices:
(Gratitude Journaling/Affirmations/Vision
Board etc)
_____

Other Self-Care: (Example: doctor visit,
pedicure, relaxed, baseball game, time with
friends, time with pet)

_____
_____

Today's Reflection: (Focus on lessons & gems)

_____
_____
_____
_____
_____
_____
_____
_____
_____
_____
_____
_____
_____
_____
_____
_____
_____
_____
_____
_____
_____

Date _____   _____

Supplements/Vitamins/Medications:

_____

_____

Fitness/Cardio: (30 min suggested)

_____

Deep Breathing/Body Stretching/Laughing:

_____

Spirituality: (Meditation/Prayer etc)

_____

Mind/Brain: (Reading/Writing/Journaling etc)

_____

Nature or Green Space:

_____

Hydration: (how much?)

_____

Sleep: (6-8 hours suggested)(How long?)

_____

Self-Tenderness/Self-Nurturing: (Self-hug and
say I love you, to you!, Say kind things to self)

_____

Positive Mindset/Manifesting Practices:
(Gratitude Journaling/Affirmations/Vision
Board etc)

_____

Other Self-Care: (Example: doctor visit,
pedicure, relaxed, baseball game, time with
friends, time with pet)

_____

_____

Today's Reflection: (Focus on lessons & gems)

_____
_____
_____
_____
_____
_____
_____
_____
_____
_____
_____
_____
_____
_____
_____
_____
_____
_____
_____
_____
_____
_____
_____

Date _____   _____

Supplements/Vitamins/Medications:

_____

_____
Fitness/Cardio: (30 min suggested)

_____
Deep Breathing/Body Stretching/Laughing:

_____
Spirituality: (Meditation/Prayer etc)

_____
Mind/Brain: (Reading/Writing/Journaling etc)

_____
Nature or Green Space:

_____
Hydration: (how much?)

_____
Sleep: (6-8 hours suggested)(How long?)

_____
Self-Tenderness/Self-Nurturing: (Self-hug and
say I love you, to you!, Say kind things to self)

_____
Positive Mindset/Manifesting Practices:
(Gratitude Journaling/Affirmations/Vision
Board etc)

_____
Other Self-Care: (Example: doctor visit,
pedicure, relaxed, baseball game, time with
friends, time with pet)

_____

_____

Today's Reflection: (Focus on lessons & gems)

_____
_____
_____
_____
_____
_____
_____
_____
_____
_____
_____
_____
_____
_____
_____
_____
_____
_____
_____
_____
_____
_____

Date _____   _____

Supplements/Vitamins/Medications:

_____

_____
Fitness/Cardio: (30 min suggested)

_____
Deep Breathing/Body Stretching/Laughing:

_____
Spirituality: (Meditation/Prayer etc)

_____
Mind/Brain: (Reading/Writing/Journaling etc)

_____
Nature or Green Space:

_____
Hydration: (how much?)

_____
Sleep: (6-8 hours suggested)(How long?)

_____
Self-Tenderness/Self-Nurturing: (Self-hug and
say I love you, to you!, Say kind things to self)

_____
Positive Mindset/Manifesting Practices:
(Gratitude Journaling/Affirmations/Vision
Board etc)

_____
Other Self-Care: (Example: doctor visit,
pedicure, relaxed, baseball game, time with
friends, time with pet)

_____

_____

Today's Reflection: (Focus on lessons & gems)

_____

_____

_____

_____

_____

_____

_____

_____

_____

_____

_____

_____

_____

_____

_____

_____

_____

_____

_____

_____

_____

_____

_____

Date _____   _____

Supplements/Vitamins/Medications:

_____

_____
Fitness/Cardio: (30 min suggested)

_____
Deep Breathing/Body Stretching/Laughing:

_____
Spirituality: (Meditation/Prayer etc)

_____
Mind/Brain: (Reading/Writing/Journaling etc)

_____
Nature or Green Space:

_____
Hydration: (how much?)

_____
Sleep: (6-8 hours suggested)(How long?)

_____
Self-Tenderness/Self-Nurturing: (Self-hug and say I love you, to you!, Say kind things to self)

_____
Positive Mindset/Manifesting Practices: (Gratitude Journaling/Affirmations/Vision Board etc)

_____
Other Self-Care: (Example: doctor visit, pedicure, relaxed, baseball game, time with friends, time with pet)

_____

_____

Today's Reflection: (Focus on lessons & gems)

_____

_____

_____

_____

_____

_____

_____

_____

_____

_____

_____

_____

_____

_____

_____

_____

_____

_____

_____

_____

_____

Date _____ _____

Supplements/Vitamins/Medications:
_____
_____

Fitness/Cardio: (30 min suggested)
_____

Deep Breathing/Body Stretching/Laughing:
_____

Spirituality: (Meditation/Prayer etc)
_____

Mind/Brain: (Reading/Writing/Journaling etc)
_____

Nature or Green Space:
_____

Hydration: (how much?)
_____

Sleep: (6-8 hours suggested)(How long?)
_____

Self-Tenderness/Self-Nurturing: (Self-hug and
say I love you, to you!, Say kind things to self)
_____

Positive Mindset/Manifesting Practices:
(Gratitude Journaling/Affirmations/Vision
Board etc)
_____

Other Self-Care: (Example: doctor visit,
pedicure, relaxed, baseball game, time with
friends, time with pet)

_____
_____

Today's Reflection: (Focus on lessons & gems)

_____

_____

_____

_____

_____

_____

_____

_____

_____

_____

_____

_____

_____

_____

_____

_____

_____

_____

_____

_____

Date _____   _____

Supplements/Vitamins/Medications:

_____

_____
Fitness/Cardio: (30 min suggested)

_____
Deep Breathing/Body Stretching/Laughing:

_____
Spirituality: (Meditation/Prayer etc)

_____
Mind/Brain: (Reading/Writing/Journaling etc)

_____
Nature or Green Space:

_____
Hydration: (how much?)

_____
Sleep: (6-8 hours suggested)(How long?)

_____
Self-Tenderness/Self-Nurturing: (Self-hug and
say I love you, to you!, Say kind things to self)

_____
Positive Mindset/Manifesting Practices:
(Gratitude Journaling/Affirmations/Vision
Board etc)

_____
Other Self-Care: (Example: doctor visit,
pedicure, relaxed, baseball game, time with
friends, time with pet)

_____

_____

Today's Reflection: (Focus on lessons & gems)

_____

_____

_____

_____

_____

_____

_____

_____

_____

_____

_____

_____

_____

_____

_____

_____

_____

_____

_____

_____

_____

Date _____   _____

Supplements/Vitamins/Medications:
_____
_____

Fitness/Cardio: (30 min suggested)
_____

Deep Breathing/Body Stretching/Laughing:
_____

Spirituality: (Meditation/Prayer etc)
_____

Mind/Brain: (Reading/Writing/Journaling etc)
_____

Nature or Green Space:
_____

Hydration: (how much?)
_____

Sleep: (6-8 hours suggested)(How long?)
_____

Self-Tenderness/Self-Nurturing: (Self-hug and say I love you, to you!, Say kind things to self)
_____

Positive Mindset/Manifesting Practices: (Gratitude Journaling/Affirmations/Vision Board etc)
_____

Other Self-Care: (Example: doctor visit, pedicure, relaxed, baseball game, time with friends, time with pet)
_____
_____

Today's Reflection: (Focus on lessons & gems)

_____

_____

_____

_____

_____

_____

_____

_____

_____

_____

_____

_____

_____

_____

_____

_____

_____

_____

_____

_____

_____

_____

_____

It is my hope, that by providing you this tool, it will assist you in "upping your game". In other words, I hope this tool will assist you in your process of becoming a better you, and in rising to your greatest potential. I made this tool for all of us on this quest of continually learning and growing and in the process of transforming ourselves, like the butterfly. This is the process I use, every single day. It consistently challenges me to be accountable for my own self-care. Self-Care is a term I never knew until after my health took a turn for the worse. That day in the hospital, I literally had to decide to start caring for myself, before caring for others, if I wanted to live, literally! And since then, this daily routine has helped me bring my health back and has become a tool in healing my mind and body. I created this process for myself. Now, it can assist others as I put it in this wonderful pocketbook size for everyone to use, as a part of their self-care toolkit. I hope this helps you, so it doesn't get to the mission critical state. Be Proactive! ~Author Holly, Your Joyful Guide

Visit me on the Facebook Page: *Positive Quotes with Author Holly* and *Choose Joyful with Joyful Navigations™*
Website: https://joyfulnavigations.com

Author Holly R. Dickinson is a Lightworker and a Mass Influencer of 7 million plus followers on her Facebook Page. She is a Mother of 4, now adults. She is in a loving marriage to her husband of 27 years. Early life brought many traumas and challenges to her. She shares her wisdom, perspectives, and courage in her writings. God, love, kindness, gratitude, family, awareness, courage, action, trust, compassion, forgiveness, self-care, positivity, and choosing joy are key for her.